The W
Untamea

Edited by Alan Parry

The Whiskey Tree
Edited by Alan Parry

Brought to you by The Broken Spine

Art and Literature

ISBN: 9798870589800

© Alan Parry, 2023. All rights reserved.

Book design: Alan Parry and Andrew James Lloyd
Cover Image: MidJourney
Cover Composition: Andrew James Lloyd
Edited by Alan Parry
All copyright to individual texts are held and reserved
by the authors

The Broken Spine Ltd
Southport / England / United Kingdom
www.thebrokenspine.co.uk

'Poets, come out of your closets, open your windows, open your doors, You have been holed up too long in your closed worlds'

Lawrence Ferlinghetti

The Whiskey Tree

Untamed Nature Poetry

Edited by Alan Parry

Contents

1	*Mother of Seas*	- Alan Parry
2	*A North Mayo Blessing*	- Anne Walsh Donnelly
3	*Doghouse*	- Jay Rafferty
4	*Cutting the Turf*	- David Butler
5	*Desert Antlers*	- Sue Finch
6	*Olmec Crocodile: Cipactli*	- Karen Pierce Gonzalez
8	*Your Mother Stands on the North-East Side of the House*	- Morag Anderson
9	*The Great Desertification*	- Vikki C.
10	*Larks Attending*	- Mary Earnshaw
13	*Sup a Well Earned*	- Paul Brookes
14	*Allochory*	- Cáit O'Neill McCullagh
16	*Now and Forever*	- Matthew M. C. Smith

18   *I am the Lamb that Roams the Land*
                         - James Jackson

20   *Night Theatre*
                         - Paul Robert Mullen

21   *Recommended Reading*

22   *Advance Praise*

Mother of Seas
Alan Parry

for cowards & the corrupt
for heretics & hedonists
for liars & thieves

for men who throw their mothers into the blue

standing in the dying sun
miles from shore - on the squint of the horizon
where waters creep
through the floorboards
& the ceiling is stars

between the waves / among the waves
Aivazovsky's deep sea
dreams

denial becomes frothing saltwater rum
& as men of streets drink
titanic waves grow
& crash
through windows

anemones crawl along bars
between barnacles
seeking shelter

outside
under glossy pregnant moon
coral women with fish tails strike
depraved poses

women are rocks
women are dead mothers

women are ocean

A North Mayo Blessing
Anne Walsh Donnelly

May your loved ones rest in the ledges of your heart
just as puffins and kittiwakes nest in Dún Briste,

May you feel their breath in the breeze
that blows in from Blacksod Bay.

May you hear them in the laughter of grey seals
and children playing tag on the beach.

May they lie beside you on soft tufts of grass
in meadows of dog-violet, foxglove and red clover.

May they cling to the soles of your feet like grains
of sand when you walk on Cross Beach.

May you stand on the shore, saltwater mixing with tears
and trust they will always be with you.

Doghouse
Jay Rafferty

The red soil, the too-yellow-green scrub. Martian
to the eye at first. By the roadside, a loch of dry dead
planks and a smattering of roof tiles (grey or brown)
and, in the middle of it all, a golden pear, a dog,
like a sack of onions. Colorado stray, her snout/stem
curling towards the remnants of a fireplace's grate,
the chimney now a piazza more than a spout.

Cicada cries, cricket tunes, grasshoppers as big
as your forefinger, never mind the cars tearing past.
It would be hard enough to sleep through the invertebrate
racket. In the glimpse of the rubble though, the memory
that blurred past was a butter yellow tail sweeping
the planks. The cur's tail curtailing her screeching
alarm clocks, one grey-green forefinger at a time.

Cutting the Turf
David Butler

A High lodged in the pocket of Dogger
is holding at bay the Atlantic fronts.
All day, the machinery's rattle has laid
marla rails over yielding earth, ridged
to the hide of a crocodile. Later,
hatchbacks gather, haggle, guess
the harvest of fibrous loaves: how wind-
blown drills will stack up; box-braids
on the scalp of the drying bog.

Desert Antlers
Sue Finch

Standing at the edge of the desert
I saw greyed antlers on the sand.
All the way there I had imagined
an orangey-yellow expanse,
painted it in my mind over and over again.
Paler, faded, it stretched out,
on and on and on; a shade of ochre.
Doubled by their shadow the antlers begged
for the touch of my fingers.

You said we would die if we tried to go across.
Your hand on my shoulder halted my movement.
I couldn't decide whether to ignore your touch
or turn back to you.
It was as if someone had paused time
and everything depended on my next steps.

Crying, I reached out for the bones.

Olmec Crocodile: Cipactli
Karen Pierce Gonzalez

I

Tricked out of the primordial sea~
with promises of divinity
by four gods of direction,
I was birthed from water into beast,
scraped against craggy rock beds,
cracking open the blisters of having been forced
to fall apart for your forests, peaks, and valley floors
flat enough to build god-temples on.

Mouth open, my rains anoint
the top of your bobbled heads,
dilute appetites whet for more
ferocious shorelines of day
until only shadowlands exist
on a battlefield of reptilian desires
spawned in brain stems that don't blink
at the sight of spilt blood.

II

Midair, I dream-swim an ancient ocean
behind a steel blue rack of sky.
Torn leg joints leak brine
unable to wash wounds clean.
I am fettered against my will,
with you in a twisted jute net
sewn onto my leathery hide.

Tasked to raise your heaven up
by the roots with my curved teeth
—still longing to bite into plankton mud—
I tire; turn my thick skeletal back
on the deities you pray to.

III

I seal my eyes and lips to stop the slide
of tears from becoming a flood.
I do not want to drown the yellow marigolds
sprouting from the ribs of my webbed feet.
Without asking, you pluck them
for altars the first day
of each lunar lit, multi-year cycle.

Such stealing singes. Your fingertips
grasp for stems of hope that, endlessly,
I will help you out of the muck
you keep making by wanting more
than you can have –
a broken core I cannot fix.

Your Mother Stands on the North-East Side of the House
after Zaffar Kunial
Morag Anderson

Your young mother ruins her only shoes
crouching for hours in rainwater
on the north-east side of the house.
Nimbostratus bruises plume under
woollen cuffs pulled over thin wrists.
Break-blackened fingers probe beneath
split lips, explore the exposed-bone surface
in her swollen basket of teeth.

Forced to fit inside the ribs of *bitch*
whose *tc* teaches her the asylum
and deceit of a well dug di*tc*h,
the rocky ou*tc*rop's quartz defiance.

She ha*tc*hes a plan to rise from this mulch—
taller and straighter—a resurrected birch.

The Great Desertification
Vikki C.

To be made new outside this skin. Unceded before the
dazzling green. How do you open a day without dust pouring
beyond? You — a motion picture, contoured from aeons of
neglect. Every mirage finds your face in venomous romance.
Wearing a delusion of gold, we couldn't afford across trenches,
worlds that vapour abandoned.

The eagle opens its wings in sync with your dirty mind.
Below the beltline, you travel Arizona, fingering the peripheries to
hell. Press a thumb deep in a fault, so you don't forget your place.
Because your god invited me to a seance, to lie with the dust devil,
dusk tastes of lovers' blood — the ones that didn't die.

Behind my raw shoulder, a purer shade of oblivion, losing focus.
Disciples robed and sparkling, eyes watering over the wars we never
settled. Broken homes, marriages, igneous trauma. *This great crush
we could never cure.* Breaking is a continental language, its drift
uncatchable.

How many layers of us rise up as gleaming resurrections, spines
crooked, to splinter, to spread — as ivory gushing over a wide idea
of blue? Seeing you for the first time as myth, miasma, terracotta
mantra. Hallucinating your body as sustenance that might not poison
me.

The sun goes down on me different — its hot tongue, excusable.
They ask my faith. I tell them I washed my hair in the last stream,
looking up like a good woman. Admiring this hard life. Too much to
bear, to take in wholly, without choking.

Larks Attending
Mary Earnshaw

I

The fisherman's path stretches ahead,
utterly unpeopled.

Alone and unencumbered
I step along the path of stumbling stone
and mud
and tyre tracks.
Leave the scruffy dunes behind,
breathing openness,
salt marsh to either side.

A frothing, fizzing
guard of honour arises,
fluttering notes of deception.
Larks are rising in number
deterring me from their nests –
but it feels like a joyous parade,
I'm the heroine of the hour –
and my stepping turns lighter than air.

I can almost see the sky arch,
the world un-edged
slipping convexly away
as sea meets sky
somewhere
so far away
it might be legend.

Nesting grounds passed,
the guards sink back,
drop to the ground
relieved their nests remain
unplundered,
all quiet.

II

Now I hear the faint rustle:
a light breeze in salt grasses.
I see the rivulet running in,
pressed by distant, incoming waves
pulled by invisible forces –
the moon's outshone by the high sun
and gravity's never for showing.

At length the mud encroaches,
the sinking of too-light shoes says,
stay,
and I stay, gaze across the estuary,
to light winking on windows of cars
on another coastal road,
traffic seeking the old resorts,
a tower trying to touch the sky,
a great dipper raring
and curving on the golden mile.

Closer to foot lie marshes,
lush, seeming placid,
death-traps for the unwary,
sanctuary for birds and sea-plants.

A raptor swoops,
sleek and swift and dangerous,
to perch on a drifted log,
dissimulating
in hues of gold and amber.

My guards re-awaken,
rising like bubbles in lemonade,
singing their hearts
until I leave once more.

III

If that were that I'd say
it's been a good day
on the bird walk
on the salt marsh
as the straying sea hides
from the marsh it salts.

But as I near the dunes,
an interloper – a loper –
appears, almost too fast to see,
leaping its way at speed
to who knows what or where
and I, joy-filled,
spirit replenished with summer-day
nature-kissed loveliness,
slide into my car and drive
– mere human on wheels –
away.

Sup A Well Earned
Paul Brookes

pint of soil.

Let particles caress your throat.
Parch your sodden lips.

Admire the crests of dried clay
that lap the ploughed fields.

Fill a soiling can with dust
from the tap to sprinkle
your wet flowers.

Beware waterquakes
that bring down homes.

Allochory
after a painting by Paul Bloomer
Cáit O'Neill McCullagh

Before—when the gannet's eyes, un-blackened, flamed
blue—we were allochory; seed scatter for trees
no longer moved to roam the rivened till.

Once, their branches had dreamed assembling; settling
forests, braiding roots to ling & twayblade; fern-furl,
to the turning world & the many colours of water.

Moons since,

                    after the ice let loose her clasp

& drove a flint-hard ard to furrow
straths & the looped slakening of oxbows,
when the seas began to roll, unbroken; unplown,

then

           we became—

blush-plumed with strippit crowns, learning
to store sun; fatten it in acorn hearts. In the rookering,
months—when crows curl fingered wings to winnow the

Cailleach's hewn light, when naked birks bulge
with sorrowed nests—our eyes smoot at your rottening
hairst, unbaled in the misting rain, in the hammered silver

of sleet. We pity you: mouths gnarled, nets storm-ripped; lines
unburdened with fish; the fleshless beak of the bonebreaker
bird; the trembled heron skraiking her wretchery.

Fleet, we tail tip to the oak, her canopy true-ing
in colour: prasine to citrine; goldenrod; saffron burnish.

We sing the ochring of the woodland's foils; dirndls circling

from airy definition, becoming leaf melt; nurture for
a second spring. Drookit, hope softens this bed for nutfall.
& we gullet her fattening, drill & sink sweet treasuries of seed.

Lang-downy, a birch clings to her fiery tips, spears a flicker–
crown to the darkling sky. Curtaining her feet, we bury
the world's ripening. Come brambling thrush, sprout

thorny guards; blackthorn hallow a circling; let leave
for life's precarity. Harrow-ache & hollow-yearn
are ended here; windfall is unwasted,

in this, the kindness that we sow;

planting oaks like jays.

Now and Forever
Matthew M. C. Smith

We drive away from the hospital past trees and lawns
viewed through rain-lines. Cold glass mists with our breath.
I make out giant, uncut shrubs, hedgerow tops high and wily
on the exit road and a solitary fountain in the grounds, stopped.

It feels a betrayal to leave him there in the psychiatric hospital,
that gravestone monument on the wooded hill, addled in the
confusion of strangers; treachery to leave him in captivity,
walking from ward's end to end, through locked corridors
with boiling radiators, touching things, pacing, lurking and lurching
at any moment sensing draught's freedom; fumbling his pockets
for cigarettes and asking and asking.

I see his mind as a diseased honeycomb with tiny fires,
hexagons aglow. The slow flame, edged with grey, spreads
through boundless chambers, a slow exchange like a burnt, whittled
matchstick lighting touch-paper, torched up with a faint breath of air.
This time is only one time, a time unrecognised, a now that never
seems now, is never quite gone.

The car hits a rut on the road. The indicators click
and the windscreen wipers swish
at the junction's pause. We pull out
and continue to drive in silence.

Through him, with him, in him
in the unity of the Holy Spirit.
All glory and honour is yours
now and forever.

If there was sun and amber light. If he could lie
within the humming trails of a flower field;
if his stooped bones were unfurled
and every cell unburdened;
all his tiny fires put out
with the unstopping of water.

If the body could float,
be carried, suspended in mid-air
and the claret bruises
on his skull healed
and we had him
as he was,
exactly as he was

Now and forever

Amen

I Am the Lamb that Roams the Land
James Jackson

Lore.
It is not the sound that trembles on the lips
of the sycophants
all bulldozers and no brain!
It is the whip snap CRACK!
of the dead leaves
that roll and tumble
in a cacophony of warmer days.
Long forgotten, long lost.

See how the Holly King prays
His brow moist with frost
that sheds rain clouds from his skin.
It fissures the Earth,
lush greens die away again
til next season
        so we hope.

I beg questions of monarchs
but answers are sparse and disperse
as ripples in disturbed waters.
Water kisses my lip.
I am beyond salvation.
Mother! O Mother!
How I fear
the feast is of the bones
        of the woods.

I crave the soil
to fill my palms
to rush up through *my* body
thick ichorous blood
worming its way through my roots.
Great clots of loam bubbling.
Let sapling burst forth
fireworks through my skin.

My kin. O my Kin is the forest.

And all that roams between.

Night Theatre
Paul Robert Mullen

you resonate
where rivers carve narratives

stoic & unyielding
the landscape is silent

contours of me
a spectrum unbound by convention
        transparent hue

seeing you break
                away
through halflight
canyons flooded with wind
hiding secrets

untamed terrain // desolation
mountains unrestrained & sovereign
unbound by human confines

just your footprints
where freedom is unspoken law

you speak   *i had to…*

the muted luminescence
        a silent ballet

this theatre
        your sanctuary
my purgatory

        our wilderness

Recommended Reading

Anthologies

The Broken Spine Artist Collective: First Edition (2020)
The Broken Spine Artist Collective: Second Edition (2020)
The Broken Spine Artist Collective: Third Edition (2021)
The Broken Spine Artist Collective: Fourth Edition (2022)
The Broken Spine Artist Collective: Fifth Edition (2022)
BOLD: An anthology of masculinity themed creative writing (2023)

Chapbooks

Neon Ghosts (A. Parry, 2020)
The Mask (E. Horan, 2021)
Holy Things (J. Rafferty, 2022)
From This Soil (C. Bailey, 2022)
The Keeper of Aeons (M. M. C. Smith, 2022)
Four Forked Tongues (L. Aur, S. Filer, B. Lewis & E. Kemball, 2023)
Modest Raptures (E. Rees, 2023)
Surviving Death (K. Houbolt, 2023)
Twenty Seven (A. Parry, 2023)

Advance Praise

'This compelling, essential anthology maps not only the Anthropocene landscape – the world fighting back against the destructive influence of humankind - but equally importantly, the interior landscape of human thought and human emotion, rich with its own beauty, its own wildernesses. These are poems with a raw power that demands our attention. They remind us we can never be truly whole until we acknowledge the untamed landscape of the imagination within ourselves.'
- John Glenday, author of *The Golden Mean*

'Kudos to The Broken Spine for coalescing this new thematic anthology, its accumulative reset, mining and upending the pastoral tradition of landscape poetry. Each poem builds on the next, to produce new visionary territory where body/self/word are both inside and outside of nature, a wrestling with and overturning of the elements. Gritty, explosive, heartbreaking poems distil the human condition, expanding upon our relationships to emotion/environment, whether of scenes in park edges, at highway shoulders, in the cartographies of night streets and memory, in ravaged forests, or hallucinations of dying oceans. This is a soul-sourced magic book -- stark, beautiful, hopeful and groundbreaking!'
- Robert Frede Kenter, author of *Audacity of Form*

'Alan Parry has curated an extraordinary collection of poems and poets in Whiskey Tree: Untamed Nature. With writers of such quality and accomplishment—Morag Anderson, Vicki C., Anne Walsh Donnelly, Karen Pierce Gonzales, and Matthew M.C. Smith—it's such a rich well. There's fire here. And ice. Ocean shore and highland. There's heart, and there's space. The real strength of the collection, though, is its range of voice and vision. These poets each offer their own gifts with clarity and with depth. Each page reveals necessary truths. Each extends its own invitation to reunite with our natural world, with the beauty all around us. And for these gifts, for these poets, I couldn't be more grateful.'
- Jack B. Bedell, Poet Laureate of Louisiana, 2017-2019

'Nature poetry that avoids the obvious and demands to be explored in depth.'
- Henry Normal, author of *The Fire Hills*

Printed in Great Britain
by Amazon